# Obvious Adams

## The Story of a Successful Business Man

D1596609

# By Robert R. Updegrafft

## Foreword and Afterword by
## John Brubaker

Library of Congress Control Number: 2019930829

ISBN: 978-0-9850671-8-2

Printed in the United States of America

# Praise For Obvious Adams

"The young man who is going to seek his fortune in the advertising business should have Obvious Adams for a handbook. Indeed, any young man who is going to seek his fortune in anything might be aided by the common sense and business acumen displayed in this little volume."

- *The New York Times*

# Foreword

*Dr. Watson walks into a room, and Sherlock Holmes instantly accuses him of hanging out in the club all day.*

*"How did you know?" Watson asks.*

*"A gentleman goes forth on a showery and miry day. He returns immaculate in the evening with the gloss still on his hat and his boots. Is it not obvious?" Holmes says.*

*"Well, it is rather obvious," Watson admits.*

*"The world is full of obvious things which nobody ever observes," says Holmes.*

*(The Hounds of The Baskervilles, Conan Doyle)*

Have you ever missed something because it was too obvious? It was right in front of you, staring you in the face? I don't know how many times I've frantically searched for my "lost" sunglasses only to eventually find them on my head. Or my "lost" keys that were actually in the ignition of the car. Talk about overlooking the obvious.

It may not be obvious until after you read and absorb it, but you're holding in your hands a magnificent gift. I should add the disclaimer that to reap the benefits you need to apply the wisdom.

As a matter of fact, this might be the best book you've never heard of.

Published in 1916, this story is over a hundred years old, yet its message is just as relevant today as it was in 1916. Perhaps even more so.

Why? Because never in the history of our society have we had greater access to information yet at the same time we've never been more deficient in common sense.

Advertising legend David Ogilvy believed this book changed his life and was so passionate about its message that he had his employees read it every year.

I've read the book a dozen times, and each time I pick up a new insight or piece of wisdom from it. It's less a book about advertising, or even about Adams himself, as much as it's a book about the power of mindset.

I encourage you to read and re-read this book a dozen times, too. I can realistically promise you that you'll glean some new wisdom from *Obvious Adams* each time you re-read it.

The author Robert Updegrafft was born in 1889 and was in my humble (but very accurate) opinion one of the original business coaches, well before the term became popular. He was the personal coach to executives at some of the leading companies of his era. Firms like Aluminum Company of America, American Brake Shoe Company, General Foods, John Hancock, Kellogg Company, and Westinghouse Electric benefitted from his example and instruction.

How impactful is Updegraff's work? *New York Times* best-selling author and marketing genius Jack Trout calls *Obvious Adams* the best book on marketing that he has ever read. While you may be thinking "but I'm not in marketing," that couldn't be further from the truth. Regardless of occupation or industry we are all in some way, shape, or form *marketers*.

The beauty of this book is that there's no "business speak" in it. So, if you're looking for pie charts, graphs, or a bunch of management jargon and buzzwords you'll be disappointed. *Obvious Adams* is just 40 pages long and reads so easily it's like you're simply having a conversation with an old friend over a cup of coffee.

# Obvious: (adjective) easily discovered, seen, or understood

The *Oxford Dictionary* defines obvious as "easily perceived or understood; clear, self-evident, or apparent." The only problem is that often the obvious doesn't appear so obvious because people are searching for complexity. Too many leaders, managers, executives, and coaches think solving a problem should require a complicated solution.

Look no further than the health and nutrition industry. There are lots of complicated diets, fads and trendy programs, but the one true, battle-tested weight loss solution is to simply consume fewer calories than you burn each day. Seems obvious enough, right?

Sadly, common sense isn't common practice because we think, "there must be more to it than that." Actually, no. I'm pretty sure what caused your weight gain in the first place was consuming more calories than you burned each day.

As a society we like complex solutions because we think if something has more steps, involves processes, or costs more then it must be better.

**We tend to complicate winning whether it's in the locker room or the board room.**

As a result, we often miss out on hidden opportunities because they're "hidden out in the open". In other words, we are overlooking the obvious.

**Thinking inside the box can be a good thing.**

Sometimes the answers we are looking for are simple, but we as humans have a propensity for complicating things unnecessarily. Simple strategies can rapidly transform your results.

If you're wondering about missing out on the obvious, or you know you're guilty of this, don't worry. It's not your fault. Our brains often naturally miss the obvious for some important reasons. There's so many stimuli in our world today that we miss a lot of things. Our brains have evolved to process the minimum in order to maintain our survival and filter out what it deems as trivial. If a sabre tooth tiger was chasing someone; that person's brain wouldn't notice a rare flower on the ground while he ran for his life.

In what's known as the famous Invisible Gorilla Study, psychologists Christopher Chabris and Daniel Simons had volunteers watch a video where two groups of people — some dressed in white, some in black — passed basketballs around. The volunteers were told to count the passes among players dressed in white while ignoring the passes of those in black.

The participants were so focused on the task of counting passes that they failed to notice something incredibly obvious: a man in a gorilla suit walking through the middle of the court, in very close proximity to the participants.

In another experiment, Chabris and Simons staged a fake fight along an outdoor path and had subjects run past the scene of the fight while chasing someone. According to Chabris, many didn't notice the fight. You might think they would notice something as obvious as people fighting right in front of them, but they didn't.

The fact of the matter is that what "should" grab your attention doesn't if you're focused on an alternate task like counting passes or chasing a suspect. The concept is known as **inattentional blindness**. It happens to us because humans are complex beings, and we can focus inwardly while performing tasks outwardly. Anyone who has ever walked through a crowded airport while texting on his or her phone and walked right past the correct gate can attest to this.

Enjoy reading the book. I'm confident it will change your perspective and have you viewing your craft through a very different lens.

John Brubaker
CoachBru.com

A lone man sat at a table by a window in the Dickens Room of the Tip Top Inn, Chicago. He had finished his dinner and was apparently waiting for his black coffee to be served.

Two men entered and were shown to a table nearby. Presently one of them glanced at the man by the window.

"See that man over there?" he whispered to his companion.

"Yes," said the latter, looking disinterestedly in the direction indicated.

"Well, that is Obvious Adams."

"Is that so?" And he almost turned in his chair this time to get a good look at the most-talked-of man in the advertising business. "Ordinary-looking man, isn't he?"

"Yes, to look at him you would never think he was the famous Obvious Adams of the biggest advertising agency in New York. And to tell the truth, I can't see why he is such a little tin god in the business world."

"I've heard him speak two or three times at the Ad league meetings, but he never said anything that we didn't know already. He seems to have a lot of people buffaloed, though. I confess he was a disappointment to me."

It is funny, but that is the way most outsiders talk about Adams. And yet this same Adams has been an important factor in the success of more well-known businesses than perhaps any other one man.

Even at this moment, while the two men were talking about him, he was making business history. He had turned the menu card face down and was drawing lines and making notes on the back. To anyone looking over his shoulder the result of his work would have been meaningless, but it seemed to please Adams, for he nodded his head earnestly to himself and put the menu into his pocket as the obsequious waiter came to help him into his overcoat.

Half an hour later a telephone bell jingled in the library of a sumptuous home in an Iowa city. It rang a second time before the man lounging in the big mahogany chair in front of the fireplace arose and picked up the receiver.

"Hello!" he snapped, and he scowled at the intrusion. "Hello! Hello! Oh, it's you, Mr. Adams. I didn't expect to hear from you so soon. Where are you?

Chicago? You've got a plan? You have? Well, I've just been sitting here thinking about it myself, and I've chewed three cigars to a pulp trying to figure out what we ought to do about it."

Then silence in the sumptuous library. Then a series of what sounded like approving grunts.

"I see your idea. Yes, I think they will do it, all right! I'm sure they will they've got to. It's a bully idea and I believe it will turn the trick! All right; take the night train and I'll send my car down to the station to meet you in the morning. Good night."

For a long minute the man in the library stood and looked into the fireplace thoughtfully. "Now, why in thunder couldn't some of us have thought of that? It's the most natural thing in the world to do, but we had to bring a man clear from New York to show us. That Adams is a wonder, anyway!" And having addressed these remarks to the andirons, he pulled out a fourth cigar, which he smoked.

But that is another story. We are beginning back end to. To know Obvious Adams, and to understand the secret of his success, we must begin at the front end of his life. It is interesting, this story of a poor boy who began life as Oliver B. Adams in a little grocery store in a small New England town, and has grown to be known everywhere in the business world as "Obvious Adams."

It seems that Adams came of very poor, hard-working parents, that he had only a meager country-school education, and that when Oliver was twelve years of age his father died and he started working in a grocery store. He was a very ordinary sort of boy. He had no particular initiative and he seldom had any particularly bright ideas, and yet in some strange way business grew steadily in that store, and it continued to grow year by year. Anyone who knew old Ned Snow, the grocer, would tell you that none of the growth was his fault, for he was not of the growing kind—unless you mean ingrowing. Well, things ran along uneventfully until old Snow was taken ill and died. Then the store was sold out and Oliver was without a job.

The next six years of Adams' life no one knows much about but he, and of these years he has little to say. When the grocery store was sold out he took what little money he had been able to save up and went to New York, where he worked by day in a public market and went to night school in the evenings.

Then one day something happened. Near the end of his final year at night school the principal arranged for a series of educational talks for the benefit of the older students. The first of the talks was by James B. Oswald, president of the famous Oswald Advertising Agency. In those days Oswald was in his prime, and he was a most interesting and instructive talker, with a way of fitting his message to the needs of his hearers which was probably why he was successful as an advertising man. Young Oliver Adams sat spellbound throughout the talk. It was his first vision of the big world of business, and it seemed to him that Oswald was about the most wonderful man he ever had met for he actually did meet and shake hands with him after the lecture.

On the way home he thought over what Mr. Oswald had told of the advertising business. As he prepared for bed in his little third-floor rear he thought over the man Oswald and decided that he must be a fine man. As he pulled the blanket up over him and nestled down into the pillows he decided that he would like to work in the advertising business. And as he slipped off to sleep he assured himself that he would like to work for such a man as James B. Oswald.

The next morning when he awoke the last two thoughts had become united: He would like to work in the advertising business—for James B. Oswald, the natural thing to do then—to Oliver Adams, at least—was to go and tell that gentleman. Though the idea frightened him a little, it never occurred to him for a minute but that he should do just that. And so at two o'clock that afternoon he asked for two hours off at the market, that being the quiet time of day, and, after carefully blacking his shoes and brushing his clothes, started out for the big office-building which housed the Oswald Advertising Agency.

Mr. Oswald was busy, he was informed by the girl in the reception hall who had telephoned his name in to the big man.

Oliver thought a minute. "Tell him I can wait an hour and ten minutes."

The girl looked surprised, for people were not in the habit of sending such messages to the big chief. But there was something in the simple directness of the lad that seemed to make the message a perfectly natural one.

Rather to her own surprise, she repeated the message to the president precisely as she had received it.

"He will see you in about twenty minutes she announced.

Of the interview itself James Oswald used to delight to tell:

"In walked young Adams, as serious as a deacon. I didn't recognize him as one of the young men I had met the night before until he introduced himself and mentioned our meeting. Then he went on to say that he had thought the matter over and had decided that he wanted to get into the advertising business and that he wanted to work for me, and so here he was.

"I looked him over. He was a very ordinary-looking boy, it seemed to me, rather stolid, not especially bright in appearance. Then I asked him some questions to see how quick-witted he was. He answered them all readily enough, but his answers weren't particularly clever. I liked him well enough, but he seemed to lack alertness that little up-and-comingness that is necessary in advertising. And so finally I told him, in as kindly a way as possible, that I didn't think he was cut out for an advertising man and that I was very sorry, but I couldn't give him a position, and a lot more fatherly advice. It was really a choice little speech, firm but gentle.

"He took it all nicely enough. But instead of begging me to give him a chance, he thanked me for the interview and said, as he got up to go: "Well, Mr. Oswald, I have decided that I want to get into the advertising business and that I want to work for you, and I thought the obvious thing to do was to come and tell you so. You don't seem to think I could make good and so I will have to set out to find some way to prove it to you. I don't know just how I can do it, but I'll call on you again when I have found out. Thank you for your time. Good-bye." And he was gone before I could say a word.

"Well, I was set back considerably! All my little speech had been lost entirely. He didn't even entertain my verdict! I sat for five minutes thinking about it. I was rather irritated to be thus turned down by a boy, so civilly but so very definitely. All the rest of the afternoon I felt decidedly chagrined.

"That night on the way home I thought it over again. One sentence stuck in my memory: "I want to get into the advertising business and I want to work for you, and I thought the obvious thing to do was to come and tell you so."

"It all struck me in a heap: How many of us have sense enough to see and do the obvious thing? And how many of us have persistency enough in following out our ideas of what is obvious? The more I thought of it the more convinced I became that in our organization there ought to be some place for a lad who had enough sense to see the obvious thing to do and then to go about it directly, without any fuss or fireworks, and do it!

"And by George, the next morning I sent for that lad and gave him a job checking up and filing periodicals."

That was twenty years ago. Today Oliver B. Adams is the vice-president and active head of the great Oswald Advertising Agency. Old Oswald comes to the office once or twice a week and has a chat with Adams, and of course he always attends directors' meetings, but otherwise Adams is the head of the business.

It all happened naturally enough, and it all came about through that "darned obviousness," as old man Oswald good-naturedly characterizes it.

Before Adams had been working at his checking and filing job a month he went to his boss and suggested a change in the method of doing the work. His boss heard him through and then asked him what was to be gained. Adams told him that it would save about a quarter of the time and handling, and errors would be almost impossible. The change was simple and he was told to go ahead. After the new plan had been in operation three months he went to his boss again and told him that the new plan worked so well that a girl at two-thirds of his salary could take care of his work, and wasn't there something better for him? He said he noticed that the copy staff had to work nights, and he wondered if they didn't have so much work for the future that they could start in to train up a new man. The boss smiled and told him to go on back to his work. "You are no John Wanamaker." Back he went, but also he began to write copy during his spare time. The copy rush was on account of a big campaign for the California Peach Canners' Association. Adams proceeded to study up on the subject of peaches. He thought, studied, dreamed, and ate peaches, fresh, canned, and pickled. He sent for government bulletins. He spent his evenings studying canning.

One day he sat at his little desk in the checking department putting the finishing touches on an advertisement he had written and laid out. The copy chief came in to ask him for the back number of a certain paper that was in the files. Adams went to get it, leaving the advertisement on top of his desk. The copy chief's eye fell on it as he stood waiting.

"Six Minutes From Orchard To Can" was the heading. Then there were lay-outs for pictures illustrating the six operations necessary in canning the peaches, each with a little heading and a brief description of the process:

**CALIFORNIA SUN-RIPENED PEACHES**

**Picked ripe from the trees.**

**Sorted by girls in clean white uniforms.**

**Peeled and packed into the cans by sanitary machines.**

**Cooked by clean live steam.**

**Sealed air-tight.**

**Sent to your grocer for you—at 30 cents a can.**

The copy chief read the ad through and then he read it through again. When Adams got back to his desk the copy chief—Howland by name—was gone. So was the advertisement. In the front office Howland was talking with the president, and they were both looking at an ad lay-out on the president's desk.

"I tell you, Mr. Oswald, I believe that lad has the making of a copy man. He's not clever and goodness knows we have too many clever men in the shop already but he seems to see the essential points and he puts them down clearly. To tell the truth, he has said something that we up-stairs have been trying to say for a week, and it has taken us three half-page ads to say it. I wish you'd apprentice that boy to me for a while. I'd like to see what's in him."

"By George! I'll do it," agreed Mr. Oswald, whereupon he sent for Adams' boss.

"Could you get along without Adams, Mr. Wilcox?" he asked.

Mr. Wilcox smiled. "Why, yes, I guess so. He told me the other day that a girl at two-thirds his salary could do his work."

"All right; send him up to Mr. Howland."

And up Adams went to the copy department. His canned-peach copy had to be polished up, but this was given to one of the crack men, for there was need of haste, and Adams was given another subject to write on. His first attempts were pretty crude, and after several weeks the copy chief almost came to the conclusion that maybe he was mistaken in Adams, after all. Indeed, many uneventful weeks passed. Then one day a new account was landed by the Oswald Agency. It was for a package cake which was sold through grocers. The firm had limited distribution, but it had been stung by the advertising bee; it wanted to grow faster. The company was working within a fifty-mile radius of New York. Before any orders came through to the copy department some of the copy men got wind of it, and Adams heard them talking about it. That day he spent his noon hour looking up a grocery that sold the cake. He bought one of the cakes and ate a liberal portion of it as his lunch. It was good.

That night when he went home he sat down and worked on the cake problem. Far into the night the gas burned up in the little third-floor-rear room. Adams had made up his mind that if he had a chance at any of the cake copy he was going to make good on it.

The next morning the cake business came through to the copy-room. To Adams's great disappointment it was given to one of the older men. He thought the matter over all morning, and by noon he had decided that he was a chump for ever thinking that they would trust such copy to a kid like himself. But he decided to keep working on that cake account during his spare time just as though it were his account.

Three weeks later the campaign opened up. When Adams saw the proofs of the first cake copy his heart sank. What copy! It fairly made one's mouth water! Preston was famous for food-product copy, but he had outdone himself on this cake. Adams felt completely discouraged. Never would he be able to write such copy, not in a million years! Why, that copy was literature. It took mere cake at fifteen cents the loaf and made it fit food for angels. The campaign was mapped out for six months, and Adams carefully watched each advertisement, mentally resolving that he was going to school to that man Preston in the matter of copy.

Four months later, in spite of the wonderful copy running in the newspapers, both city and suburban, there were mutterings of dissatisfaction coming from the Golden Brown Cake Company. They liked the advertising; they agreed that it was the best cake advertising that had ever been done; it was increasing the business somewhat but sales were not picking up as they had anticipated. At the end of another month they were more disappointed than ever, and finally, at the expiration of the six months, they announced that they would discontinue advertising; it was not as profitable as they had hoped.

Adams felt as keenly disappointed as though he had been Mr. Oswald himself. He had become very much interested in that cake business. On the night he heard of the decision of the Golden Brown Cake Company to stop advertising he went home downcast. That evening he sat in his room thinking about Golden Brown Cake. After a while he went to a drawer and took out a big envelope containing the ads he had written for the cake months before.

He read them over; they sounded very homely after reading Preston's copy. Then he looked over some street-car cards he had laid out for his imaginary cake campaign. After that he assembled a new carton he had drawn out and colored with water-colors.

He sat and looked at these things and thought and thought and thought. Then he fell to work revising his work of months before, polishing it up and making little changes here and there. As he worked his ideas began to develop.

It was nearly three o'clock when he finally turned out his light and went to bed. The next morning he went to the office with his mind firmly made up as to what he should do.

At ten o'clock he telephoned the front office and asked if he might come down and see Mr. Oswald. He was told to come ahead.

At eleven o'clock Mr. Oswald looked up from the last piece of copy for Adams' cake campaign and smiled.

"Adams," he said, "I believe you have hit it. We have been doing wonderful cake advertising, but we have overlooked the very things you have pointed out in your plan. We have done too much advertising and not enough selling. I believe that with this plan I can go down and get that crowd back into the fold."

At three o'clock Adams was summoned to the president's office.

"Mr. Adams," said Mr. Oswald, as he sat down, "the Golden Brown Cake Company is back with us, and with us strong. They say the plan looks good to them. So we are off for another campaign. Now I want you to take this material up to Mr. Howland and go over it with him. I have told him about it, and he is just as pleased as I to think you have done it. I have told him to go over the copy with you. It is good copy, very good, but it is rough in spots, as you doubtless realize, and Mr. Howland can help you polish it up. Don't let this give you a swelled head, though, young man. It takes more than one battle to make a campaign.

Adams was treading on air when he left the president's office, but after he had talked with the copy chief for an hour he was back on earth again, for he saw that there was much to be done before the copy would be fit to print. However, his main ideas were to be followed out. They all agreed with him in his contention that people ought to taste the cake, and that to supply grocers with sample slices wrapped in oiled paper fresh every day for three weeks, to give to their customers, was a good idea; that his idea of showing the cake in natural colors in the street-car cards where it would, as he expressed it, "make people's mouths water," was a good move; that giving up their old green package in favor of a tempting cake-brown carton with rich dark-brown lettering would make for better display and appeal to the eye and the appetite. Some of these things Adams had learned back in the little New England grocery-store, and they seemed to him perfectly natural things to do. They seemed so to Mr. Oswald and Mr. Howland and all the rest when they heard the plan, and every one of them wondered why he had not thought of them.

Before the first week of the sampling campaign was up the sales had begun to show a substantial increase, and at the end of a month the Golden Brown Cake Company reported an increase of nearly thirty per cent, in their business in what was ordinarily the dullest month of the year. And that marked the beginning of one of the most successful local campaigns the Oswald Agency ever conducted. Yes, the copy was simple almost homely, in fact but it had the flavor of the old New England kitchen on baking-day, and it told of the clean, sunny bakery where Golden Brown Cakes were baked. In fact, it told it all so simply that it is entirely probable that it would have been turned down flat had not the previous campaign failed.

Several months later there was a very important conference in the front office of the Oswald Advertising Agency. The officers of the Monarch Hat Company were closeted with the president and the copy chief. Conversation, sales reports, and cigar smoke were consumed in about equal parts for nearly three hours. It seemed that the Monarch Hat Company had two retail stores in a large Southern city; that one of these stores was paying, though the other ran behind steadily. They did not want to abandon either store, for the city was large enough to support two stores, but they could not afford to go on losing. Already they had sunk hundreds of dollars in a special advertising campaign which made the prospering store prosper even more, but did not pull the unprofitable store out of the loss column. Something had to be done, and done quickly.

The conference had lasted until nearly lunch-time, but nothing had come out of it. Every plan that was suggested had either been tried or was impracticable.

"Well, gentlemen," said Mr. Oswald at last, "we have spent three hours talking about what ought to be done, whereas it strikes me that our first job is to find out what is the matter. Will you give me two weeks to find out what the matter is, and then meet for another conference?"

They were all hungry; they were talked out; yes, they would agree.

"What's your idea?" asked the copy chief, after the crowd had left.

Mr. Oswald looked at him quite seriously. "Howland, I'm going to gamble. If I could spare the time I'd go down there myself and investigate, but I can't. The Monarch people need never know about it, but we are going to send a boy down to that burg to see if he can find out what's the matter."

"You don't mean..."

"Yes, we're going to send young Adams. I have a sneaking suspicion that there is something obviously wrong in that situation—something

29

that has nothing to do with sales reports or turnover—and if there is, by cracky! I'll gamble that plain, every-day young man will ferret it out. 'Obvious' seems to be his middle name! Maybe I'm a fool, but I'm going to try it."

"Adams," said the president, as the young man stood before him, "the Monarch Hat Company has two stores, one of them is paying and the other is not. I want you to go down there and find out—without asking, mind you— which of the stores is not paying, and then I want you to find out why. Get some expense money from the cashier and leave in the morning. Come back when you feel reasonably sure you know the answer."

Adams went. He went directly to a hotel when he struck town, registered, and left his grip. Then he looked up the addresses of the two Monarch stores. Twenty minutes later he had found one store, located on the corner of two prominent streets, with a prominent entrance and display windows on both streets. The other store he found three-quarters of an hour later, right on Market Street, the main retail store street of the city, also located on a corner. But Adams was surprised, when he found the store, to discover that he had passed it three times while he was looking for it!

He stood on the opposite corner and looked at the store. It had only a very narrow front on Market Street, but a very large display window on the intersecting-street side. He stood thinking. It struck him that that store was too hard to find. What if they did do heavy advertising—the other store would reap the benefit because it was so prominently located, even though not right on Market Street. Yes, he felt sure this was the unprofitable store.

As he stood watching the store he began to notice that more people went up on that side of the street, which meant that as they approached the store their eyes were focused ahead, watching for the crossing policeman's signal to cross, and as they did cross the intersecting street their backs were turned to the big side window. And even those who came down on that side of the street did not get a good view of the window because they were on the outside of the sidewalk, with a stream of people between them and the store.

He counted the people for periods of five minutes and found that nearly fifty percent more were going up on that side than were going down. Then he counted the passers on the other side and found that nearly fifty percent more were going down on that side. Clearly that store was paying almost twice as much rent for that side display window as it should, and Market Street rent must be enormous. People didn't see the store; people couldn't find the store easily.

That night he thought, figured, and drew diagrams in his hotel room. His theory seemed to hold water; he felt sure that he was right. The next night, after having studied the situation another day and obtained some rent and sale figures from the store manager, he took a sleeper back to New York.

A few months later, as soon as the lease expired, that store moved. Adams had solved the riddle. It was really quite simple—when you knew the answer.

"It's that everlasting obviousness in Adams that I banked on. He doesn't get carried away from the facts; he just looks them squarely in the face and then proceeds to analyze, and that is half of the battle." Thus spoke Mr. Oswald to the copy chief.

That was the beginning of a series of incidents that sent Adams right to the front in the Oswald Agency and led eventually to his owning an interest. There was nothing spectacular about any of them. They were simply horse sense analyses of situations, and then more horse sense in the working out of a plan.

Came a letter—from a manufacturer of, let us say, bond papers it really was not bond papers, but I must not tell you what it was, and bond papers will do very nicely for the purpose of the story. Well, came this letter saying that they were interested in advertising and they wondered if some man from the Oswald Agency wouldn't come out to their mill and talk it over with them. As it happened, the day the letter came Mr. Oswald was sailing for Europe at eleven o'clock. The letter came in the morning mail and Adams just happened to be in the president's office when he picked it out of the basket on his desk.

"How'd you like to go out and talk to these people, Adams?" asked Mr. Oswald, with a quizzical smile, handing him the letter. He liked to try out new combinations of men and jobs.

"Oh, I'd like to," said Adams, his face lighting up with pleasure at the thought of such a mission.

"Then go, and good luck to you," said the chief, and he turned and plunged into the last-minute details of departure.

Adams went the next morning. The paper-mill president asked him if he thought bond paper could be advertised successfully. Adams replied that he couldn't tell until he knew more about the mill and the product. He had to have

33

the facts. He was given a guide, and for the next two days he fairly wallowed in paper.

He found that this mill's paper was made of selected white rags; that the purest filtered water was used in the making; that it was dried in a clean loft; and, most surprising of all, it was gone over sheet by sheet and inspected by hand. These things weren't known in those days, and Adams saw great possibilities for advertising.

The third day he spent in his hotel room laying out some tentative advertisements. These he took with him late in the afternoon and went to call on the president. The president looked them over and grunted. Plainly he was disappointed. Adams's heart sank; he was going to fail on his first selling trip, but not without a fight.

The president rocked back and forth in his chair for a few minutes. Young man," he said, finally, "every good bond paper is made of carefully selected rags"—quoting from the advertisement in his hand; "every good bond paper is made with pure filtered water; every good bond paper is loft-dried; all good papers are hand inspected. I didn't need to get an advertising man from New York to tell me that. What I wanted was some original ideas.

Everyone knows these things about bond paper."

"Why, is that so?" said Adams. "I never knew that! Our agency controls the purchase of many thousands of dollars' worth of bond papers every year, yet I venture to say that not a single man in our organization knows much about paper-making, excepting that good paper is made of rags. You see, Mr. Merritt, we aren't any of us paper-makers, and no one has ever told us these things. I know there is nothing clever about these advertisements. They are just simple statements of fact. But I honestly believe that the telling of them in a simple, straightforward way as qualities of your paper, month after month, would in a comparatively short time make people begin to think of yours as something above the ordinary among papers. You would be two or three years at least ahead of your competitors, and by the time they got round to advertising, your paper would already be entrenched in the public mind. It would be almost a synonym for the best in bond paper."

Mr. Merritt was evidently impressed by the logic of Adams's argument, yet he hesitated.

"But we should be the laughing-stock of all the paper-makers in the country if they saw us come out and talk that way about our paper, when all of the good ones make their paper that way."

Adams bent forward and looked Mr. Merritt squarely in the eyes. "Mr. Merritt, to whom are you advertising—paper-makers or paper-users?"

"I get your point," said the president. "You are right. I begin to see that advertising is not white magic, but, like everything else, just plain common sense."

And Adams went back to New York with a contract for a year's campaign, to be conducted as the Oswald Agency saw fit. The paper campaign was a success from the start. Yet, when it was analyzed, Adams had done nothing but the obvious. In due time Mr. Oswald over in Europe heard of Adams's success in securing the account, and in due time came a little note of congratulation from the president, and the thing that puzzled Adams was that the envelope was addressed to "Obvious Adams." That name "Obvious" spread all through the organization, and it stuck. Then the bond-paper campaign came into prominence, and with it Adams, and with him the new name! Today he is known among advertising men from the Atlantic to the Pacific, and it is doubtful if more than a score of them know his real name, for he always signs himself just "O.B. Adams."

Nearly every magazine you pick up shows the influence of his obviousness. In advertising Monarch Hats, for instance, they had always been shown on full-length figures of men, making the hats very small and inconspicuous.

"Let's show the hat, not the man," said Adams, one day as he looked at one of the large original photographs in the art department. "If men could see such a picture as this they would buy that hat. We lose too much when we reduce the pictures to such a small size." Whereupon he grabbed a pair of shears and sliced that perfectly good picture on all sides until there was nothing left but a hat, a smiling face, and a suggestion of a collar and neck tie. "Now" laying it on to a magazine page, which it nearly filled, "run that and put your copy in that bare left-hand corner." Nowadays you often open a magazine and find a face almost as large as your own smiling out at you and you see it, too! So, you see, Adams was really the Griffith of the advertising business, with his "close-ups." Both of them merely did the obvious thing.

Adams also discovered that advertisements did not always have to shriek out their message in two-inch type. He proved that people would read a four page advertising story, set solid in small type, if it were made interesting and dramatic like any other good story. Quite an obvious way to tell about your business, too, when you come to think of it.

You may be surprised to learn that Adams is not a particularly interesting man to meet—rather boring, in fact. He has none of the attributes commonly ascribed to genius; he is not temperamental. Since those early days he has been through many hard-fought campaigns, counseling here, directing there, holding back occasionally, making mistakes now and then, but never the same one twice. He has nursed numberless sick businesses back to health and rosy bank accounts through his skill in merchandizing. He has helped businesses to grow from loft rooms to great plants covering acres. He has altered a nation's breakfast habits. He has transformed trade names into dictionary nouns. But, for all his experience and reputation, he is rather uninteresting to meet—that is, unless you should catch him some evening in his home, as I did, and he should sit in the comfortable living-room in front of the fireplace puffing contentedly on a good cigar and soliloquizing.

It was in response to my question: "How did you come to acquire the name 'Obvious'?" that he told me some of the incidents I have just related.

"I wasn't born Obvious," he chuckled. "I had 'Obvious' thrust upon me in the old days by Mr. Oswald. I never stopped to think in those days whether a thing was obvious or not. I just did what occurred to me naturally after I had thought things over. There is no credit coming to me. I couldn't help it."

"Well," I pressed, "why don't more businessmen do the obvious, then? The men in your office say that they often spend hours trying to figure out what you are going to propose after they have decided what they think is the obvious thing to be done. And yet you fool them repeatedly."

Adams smiled. "Well," he said, "since I had that name wished upon me I have given considerable thought to that very question, and I have decided that picking out the obvious thing pre-supposes analysis, and analysis presupposes thinking, and I guess Professor Zueblin is right when he says that thinking is the hardest work many people ever have to do, and they don't like to do any more of it than they can help. They look for a royal road through some short cut in the form of a clever scheme or stunt, which they call the obvious thing to do; but calling it doesn't make it so. They don't gather all the facts and then analyze them before deciding what really is the obvious thing, and thereby they overlook the first and most obvious of all business principles. Nearly always that is the difference between the small business man and the big, successful one. Many small business men have an aggravated case of business astigmatism which could be cured if they would do the obvious thing of calling in some business specialist to correct their vision and give them a true view of their own business and methods. And that might be said of a lot of big businesses, too."

"Someday," he continued, "a lot of businessmen are going to wake up to the power and sanity of the obvious. Some have already. Theodore Vail, for instance, worried over the telegraph equipment that stood practically idle eight hours out of the twenty-four, and he conceived the night-letter idea to spread out the business over the dull hours and make more new business. What could have been more obvious?"

"Study most of the men who are getting salaries of upward of one hundred thousand dollars a year. They are nearly all doers of the obvious."

"Someday I expect to see grand opera stop advertising deficits; it is going to cease advertising opera stars, to be promptly held up in return by these same stars and advertise opera. It is going to do the obvious and advertise to the people who do not now go to opera. Then the balconies will be full and opera will pay for itself, as it should. Opera is going to come to realize that it has a legitimate merchandizing problem like hotels or books or steamship lines and that it will respond to legitimate merchandizing methods.

"Why, I even look to see the time when our municipalities will wake up to the fact that they are over-looking the obvious when they allow our great libraries, upon which we spend hundreds of thousands of dollars each year, to run along year in and year out only half fulfilling their mission, when a paltry two or three per cent, of the total appropriation spent in sane newspaper advertising to sell the library idea—the library habit, if you please—to the people would double the usefulness of our libraries to their communities. What a wonderful thing to advertise—a library! Or a great art museum!"

"The day will come, too, I think, when our railroads will get over their secrecy about fares. They will get hundreds of thousands of dollars from people who do not travel now, but who would if they realize how little it costs to travel comparatively short distances. They will publish the prices of their tickets from city to city in their time-tables not between all stations, to be sure, but between the larger places. Now instead they put their fingers to their lips and say in a whisper things such as 'Ssh!' We charge an extra fare on this train, but we are not going to tell you how much it is and you'll never guess! 'Ssh!' Why, I know a man who lived in New York for five years, and all that time he wanted to go to Philadelphia to see the city, but he never did, because he thought it cost much more than it does. He lacked the imagination to ask; but asking should not be necessary. Someday the railroads are going to do the obvious and advertise to that man. And there are hundreds of thousands of him."

At this point Mr. Adams looked at the clock. Then he excused himself while he called up his garage and ordered his car. He was leaving on the night train for Chicago to tackle a difficult situation that had developed in the business of a large client, a big breakfast-cereal manufacturer out West. They had sent for the great Adams, medicine-man of business. He would be able to prescribe the remedy.

As we rode in to the city in the luxurious limousine he sat deep in thought.

I sat and thought, too. What was the secret of this man's success, I asked myself. And then I recalled the little boy's composition on the mountains of Holland. He wrote:

The Mountains of Holland

There are no mountains in Holland.

That is the answer, I decided.

There is no secret—

It is obvious!


THE END

# Afterword

What's one of the most valuable yet underutilized educational tools? Re-reading.

As I mentioned to you in the forward, I strongly recommend you do as I have and re-read *Obvious Adams* multiple times. I share this with you for some very good reasons:

- You don't learn everything about people the first time you meet them. What makes you think you can extract all the knowledge there is to be gained the first time you read something?

- Research has shown that re-reading helps you develop a deeper understanding of what you've read.

- When you re-read something repeatedly over time, the story (and your perception of it) actually changes a bit because you've changed over time. There's an element of self-reflection in doing so.

- Simply put, it enhances your understanding of the subject matter. You appreciate details and pick up new insights and observations each time, often catching things you missed the first time around.

Perhaps the most compelling reason to reread things is the fact that there are many things competing for the attention of our subconscious mind. It's only when you re-read something repeatedly that you're able to cut through the noise and help your brain recognize a particular piece of content as more important.

This is a story of an ad man who starts from humble beginnings and rises up through the ranks to national prominence. Pretty simple, huh?

This is a story of a seemingly average guy who writes great copy that beats out established experts, yet he lacks the creativity and writing skills of his colleagues. He finds what's obvious about a situation and writes advertising copy about it.

His method seemed way too simple to produce the staggering results they did. The genius lies in the *simplicity* of his approach. Adams is proof that simple or uncomplicated truly is powerful.

### "Uncomplicating It" whatever it is, that's the $86 billion dollar question.

Why $86 billion? Because complexity comes at a cost, $86 billion dollars to be precise. That's how much money brands are leaving on the table by not simplifying, according to the 2017 Global Brand Simplicity Index.

## *Obvious Adams* Transcends Business

Life is complicated. Add in the human factor and it's even more so. When we uncomplicate it and simplify, we're happier and healthier. Phrases like "getting back to basics" and "focusing on the fundamentals" aren't just catch phrases; they are timeless truths.

The simplest global brands outperform the major indexes by 330%. This isn't just true for brand performance; it's true for us as individuals. When we "do simple better", we are happier, healthier and wealthier.

- 61% of consumers are more likely to recommend a brand because it's simple.

- 64% of consumers are willing to pay more for simpler experiences.
- 95% of employees are more likely to trust leadership at a simple workplace.

*(Research by 2017 Global Brand Simplicity Index.)*

Great leaders take the complicated and make it simple to understand in the eyes of the learner. Winning is simple; we humans tend to complicate it.

We are living in perhaps the most complicated time in human history (the external world), and the happiest and most fulfilled people are those who uncomplicate it and seek simplicity.

## How To Gain A Better Sense For The Obvious

Deliberately analyze something using just one of your senses.

Ex. Watching a speaker's body language with the volume on mute.

Ex. Watching an athlete's body language on the field or court.

Ex. Listening to the recording of a meeting with no visual context.

Eliminating one or more senses narrows your focus and helps point out the potentially obvious you may have otherwise missed due to sensory overload.

## The Lessons of *Obvious Adams*

1. Know your audience, study them, go where they go, do what they do, engage with them, ask questions, and listen.
2. Be an observer and notice how they interact (or don't) with your product or service. More importantly, understand why.
3. Do the work. Especially the work others won't.
4. Offer solutions; today, more than ever, work is being outsourced and/or automated. How do you make yourself indispensable? By offering solutions.
5. Substance beats style, and principles beat tactics.
6. Each day, spend time simply thinking. Make quiet, contemplative thought part of your daily routine.
7. Blaze your own trail. Choose yourself.
8. The power of persistence. Earning a job, earning promotion.
9. How you analyze a situation matters. At no point did you hear Adams talk about

the competition. It was always about being the best version of himself.

## How To Embrace The Concepts From *Obvious Adams*

You can begin by embracing the idea that simplicity is good, not bad. You don't need to complicate things to "add value" for clients. Simple solutions are often the best solutions. Simplicity appears to be a lost art today. Between intricate sales funnels, complex onboarding procedures, and overly detailed business plans, it's no wonder we overlook the obvious.

Conquer complexity by embracing the obvious and being very intentional about "keeping it simple," whatever "it" is. Instead of making simplicity an afterthought, deliberately make it a priority.

It's often harder to simplify something than to complicate it. So, if you want to see more simplicity, celebrate it when you see it.

## Ways To Find Simple and Obvious Solutions

1. The eight-year-old rule: Can you explain the solution to an eight-year-old child? If you can't easily explain it to a child, then it's probably too complex for anyone to easily understand.

2. Is it succinct? Can you describe it in something as short as a tweet or text message in plain English (essentially something under 2 paragraphs in length)?

3. Does it give people a "aha moment"? When you describe the answer, do they instantly light up and think, "Of course, that makes sense. Why didn't I think of that?" Take, for example, the concept of Grub Hub, the e-commerce food delivery platform. Why didn't someone else think of such an obvious and simple food delivery service before Grub Hub did in 2004?

# Final Thoughts

What might be obvious to us is often unknown to the rest of the world. For example, the business owner was well aware of the unique qualities of his company's paper, but that isn't obvious to his audience, who aren't industry experts.

There will always be details of your product or service that are obvious to you and your staff which are completely unknown to the general public. What are they for you?

Identifying them will both eliminate unnecessary complexity and prevent you from ignoring the obvious.

We often let creativity and complexity run wild to the point where we overlook the obvious because it's simple. I'm reminded of this every time I find my "lost keys" in the ignition of the car and my "lost sunglasses" on my head.

# Resources from John Brubaker

## Build a Championship Organization

If you're interested in a custom-tailored keynote speech or training program for your organization based on the principles from John Brubaker's books, contact Coach Bru at:

| | |
|---|---|
| Email: | john@coachbru.com |
| Office: | 207.576.9853 |

For hundreds of pages of free articles on leadership performance:

**CoachBru.com**

To purchase bulk copies of any of Coach Bru's books for large groups or your organization at a discount, please contact your favorite bookseller or customer service at:

**info@CoachBru.com**

# Resources from John Brubaker

## Join a Community of Game Changers

Who you are and where you'll be 5-10 years from now will be determined by the people you surround yourself with.

If you're interested in joining an exclusive group of leaders and entrepreneurs you owe it to yourself to join Coach Bru's membership community. It's the place where we turn yesterday's underdogs into tomorrow's champions.

You get 24/7 access to:

- An in-depth weekly newsletter from Coach Bru.
- A private members-only forum where you can network and interact with other members.
- Monthly group video conferences.
- Coach Bru's *Two Minute Drill* strategy videos.
- Reserved seating at all of Coach Bru's live events.
- Special pricing on Coach Bru's products and courses.
- And much more all right here at…

## YesterdaysUnderdog.com

# Books by John Brubaker

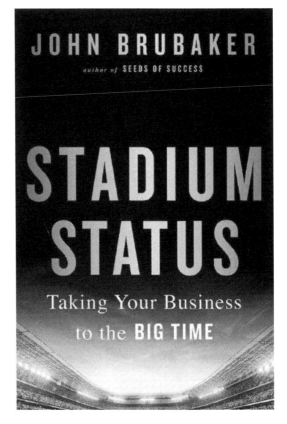

"Coach Bru views leadership performance through a very different lens, which is why we like to bring him in to speak to our organization. *Stadium Status* is indeed a unique perspective that will help you take your game to the next level."

**-Clint Hurdle,** Manager, Pittsburgh Pirates

# Also by John Brubaker

THE
SECRET
PLAYBOOK
OF COACH MORGAN RANDALL

JOHN BRUBAKER
Award-Winning Author of Seeds of Success

Special Introduction By Jack Burton

*"Shocking and provocative, John Brubaker and Coach Morgan Randall have inspired me to look at old problems with a fresh set of eyes."*

**Jeff Squires,** President, Prince Edward Island Brewing Co.

# Also by John Brubaker

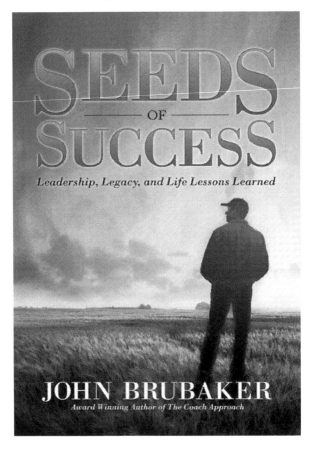

*"Coach Bru has created another slam dunk with Seeds of Success. Anyone who reads this will develop a better sense of what it takes to be a leader of significance in life's journey instead of simply chasing success."*

**Paul Biancardi,** National Recruiting Director, ESPN

# Also by John Brubaker

John Brubaker

# The Coach Approach

Success Strategies From **The Locker Room To The Board Room**

"John shares practical insights from his coaching career to teach you how to lead with your mind and your heart."

- **Jon Gordon**, *Wall Street Journal* best-selling author of *The Energy Bus* and *Training Camp*

# About the Author

John Brubaker is a nationally renowned performance consultant, speaker, and author. More importantly, he's a husband and father. John teaches audiences how to achieve stadium status results in business with straightforward tools that turbo charge performance.

Brubaker is the author of numerous books including: Amazon best-seller and #1 new release *Stadium Status*, Hollywood Book Festival award-winner *Seeds of Success*, *The*

*Secret Playbook of Coach Morgan Randall, The Daily Game Plan* and *The Coach Approach.* In 2016 his book *Seeds of Success* was adapted to a screenplay for a major motion picture.

Coach Bru has been featured on Fox Sports, ESPN Radio, CBS Radio, NBC News, Forbes, Entrepreneur and numerous other media outlets. His principles and strategies are impacting professional sports teams, corporations, universities and associations. CEO's, entrepreneurs and coaches call on Coach Bru to motivate their people. John also coaches some of the world's top executives, coaches, and athletes helping them perform their best when it matters most.

John is a graduate of Fairleigh Dickinson University with a bachelor's degree in psychology, and he also earned a master's degree in personnel psychology from FDU. Brubaker has completed his doctoral coursework in Sport Psychology at Temple University.

For more information visit:

# CoachBru.com

Made in the USA
Columbia, SC
11 February 2019